CLIMATE Change

PROBLEMS and PROGRESS

Extreme Weather

CLIMATE Change
PROBLEMS and PROGRESS

CLIMATE Change
PROBLEMS and PROGRESS

Extreme Weather

James Shoals

Mason Crest

Mason Crest
450 Parkway Drive, Suite D
Broomall, PA 19008
www.masoncrest.com

Series ISBN: 978-1-4222-4353-4
Hardback ISBN: 978-1-4222-4355-8
EBook ISBN: 978-1-4222-7450-7

First printing
1 3 5 7 9 8 6 4 2

Cover photographs by Dreamstime: Mikel Martinez De Osaba (bkgd); Trong Nguyen (right); Eric Simard (bottom). Shutterstock: Alexey Sitop (left).

Library of Congress Cataloging-in-Publication Data
Names: Shoals, James, author. Title: Extreme weather / by James Shoals.
Description: Broonmall, PA : Mason Crest, [2019] | Series: Climate challenges: problems and progress | Includes bibliographical references and index.
Identifiers: LCCN 2019013904| ISBN 9781422243558 (hardback) | ISBN 9781422243534 (series) | ISBN 9781422274507 (ebook)
Subjects: LCSH: Weather--Effect of human beings on--Juvenile literature. | Severe storms--Juvenile literature. | Climatic changes--Juvenile literature. | Natural disasters--Juvenile literature.
Classification: LCC QC863.5 .S49425 2019 | DDC 551.55--dc23 LC record available at https://lccn.loc.gov/2019013904

CONTENTS

KEY ICONS TO LOOK FOR

Words to Understand: These words with their easy-to-understand definitions will increase the reader's understanding of the text, while building vocabulary skills.

Sidebars: This boxed material within the main text allows readers to build knowledge, gain insights, explore possibilities, and broaden their perspectives by weaving together additional information to provide realistic and holistic perspectives.

Educational Videos: Readers can view videos by scanning our QR codes, providing them with additional educational content to supplement the text. Examples include news coverage, moments in history, speeches, iconic moments, and much more!

Text-Dependent Questions: These questions send the reader back to the text for more careful attention to the evidence presented here.

Research Projects: Readers are pointed toward areas of further inquiry connected to each chapter. Suggestions are provided for projects that encourage deeper research and analysis.

Series Glossary of Key Terms: This back-of-the-book glossary contains terminology used through-out this series. Words found here increase the reader's ability to read and comprehend higher-level books and articles in this field.

WORDS TO UNDERSTAND

allergen any substance that can cause an allergy

calamity an event resulting in great loss to humans and property

calving releasing of ice

cyclone a violent, rotating windstorm

desertification the process which changes habitable land into a desert; usually caused by climate change or destructive use of land

disruption the act of causing disorder

emergency a state in which some powers of public institutions are suspended for a certain period

extensively in a widespread way

famine a severe shortage of food (as through crop failure), resulting in hunger, starvation, and death

frostbite a condition in which the skin becomes frozen and loses feeling

hail pellets of frozen rain

hay fever a seasonal inflammation of the mucous membrane lining the nose, caused by an allergic reaction to pollen

hydroelectricity electricity produced by water power

hypothermia a condition in which the body temperature drops below normal

induced brought about or caused, not spontaneous

innumerous too numerous to be counted

La Niña periodic, significant cooling of the surface waters of the equatorial Pacific Ocean, which causes abnormal weather patterns

Lyme disease an acute inflammatory disease characterized by rashes, with swelling in joints, and fever, caused by a bacteria carried by the bite of a deer tick

pollen the fine spores that contain male gametes and are borne by an anther in a flowering plant

poison ivy a climbing plant with greenish flowers and white berries, which contains an irritating oil that causes a rash on contact; common in Eastern and Central United States

pollination the transfer of pollen from the anther to the stigma of a plant

precipitation the falling to earth of any form of water (rain, snow, hail, sleet, or mist)

prolonged relatively long in duration

recreational engaged in an activity as a pastime

refugee an exile who flees for safety

severe very bad in degree or extent

susceptible yielding readily to or capable of

tremor shaking or trembling

trigger to activate, release, or cause something to happen

INTRODUCTION

limate change and natural disasters, such as heat waves, droughts, floods, earthquakes, hurricanes, and thunderstorms, have been occurring since the dawn of time. But global warming is a phenomenon induced by humankind. Scientists across the world have been thoroughly examining the changing climate, and have found close links between global warming and extreme climatic events.

Global warming induced by humans has drastically altered global climatic patterns. Natural disasters that used to occur once in a hundred years are now occurring more frequently, more extensively, and with greater intensity. The destruction and damage caused by such events are also increasing. Frequent extremities in weather events are drastically affecting the global population by increasing the death toll each passing year.

Heat Wave

Heat waves occur when atmospheric temperatures rise to an unbearable level. Hot winds dry the soil, plants, and trees, causing acute shortages of water that severely affect humans and wildlife. Global warming is increasing the frequency as well as the intensity of these heat waves around the globe. Due to this, the frequency of extreme snowfall and cold winds called blizzards is decreasing in winters.

Frequency and Intensity

The World Meteorological Organization (WMO) is an agency of the United Nations (UN) that observes global climate. According to the WMO, in the next ten years heat waves would be very strong in central Asia, Australia, the western United States, and north and south Africa. It also says that although blizzards would occur less often due to global warming, their intensity would increase. Warm atmospheres hold more moisture, which causes more rain and snow. Thus, there will be extreme blizzards in winters, though at longer intervals.

Health Hazards

Human beings are most affected by extremely hot climate. They easily fall victim to diseases caused by excess heat, such as heat cramps. Heat cramps cause extreme pain in the abdomen and leg muscles, weakness, heavy sweating, and in extreme cases, vomiting followed by fainting. During heat stroke, the body temperature can rise to 40°C. If immediate medical attention is not provided, heat cramps can even cause death.

Climate Facts

• The years 2016 and 2017 were the hottest years registered by the National Aeronautics and Space Administration (NASA).

• In February 2010, North America faced an extreme blizzard, popularly known as "Snowmageddon."

Extreme Heat Waves

As predicted by scientists, with rising atmospheric temperatures, heat waves have become more severe. This prediction is beginning to come true, with increasing numbers of heat waves, one more devastating than the last.

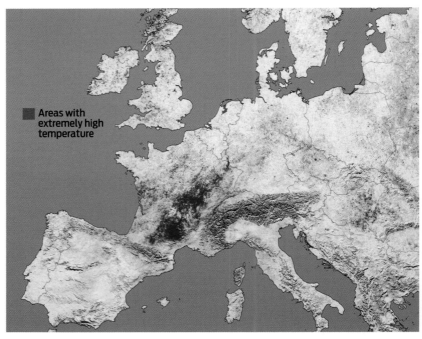

Areas with extremely high temperature

2003, Europe

Europe's deadliest heat wave in fifty years occurred in 2003. Temperatures rose up to 104°F (40°C) in July in the central and southern nations, from Germany to Turkey. The highest recorded temperature in the United Kingdom was 100.58°F (38.1°C). More than 35,000 people across the continent lost their lives. About 7,000 of these people died in Germany, 14,000 in France, almost 2,000 in the United Kingdom, and about 4,200 in Italy and Spain.

2010, Russia

From April to August 2010, Russia witnessed one of the most extreme heat waves in its one thousand years of history. Those heat waves caused extreme wildfires and droughts, killing more than fifteen thousand people. Moscow recorded above average temperatures for sixty-two days in a row, the highest being 100.04°F (37.8°C), which was far above its average temperature.

2016, North America and India

The United States recorded a major heat wave from July to October 2016. The most-affected areas included western United States, with the highest-recorded temperature of the continent being 126°F (52.2°C) in Death Valley, California.

In 2016, India faced even more terrible heat waves. On May 16, India recorded a temperature of 123.8°F (51°C) in Phalodi, in the state of Rajasthan. It was the highest temperature ever recorded in India. As of April 2017, about 4,620 deaths caused by the heat waves of the previous four years were recorded in India.

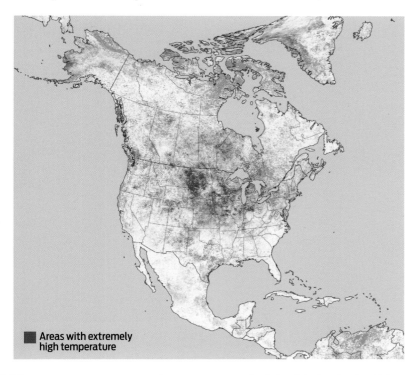

Areas with extremely high temperature

Climate Facts

• During the 2010 heat wave, temperatures in central Russia rose 18°F (10°C) above normal, killing more than 50,000 people.

• During the 2003 European heat wave, the Alpine glaciers' mass lessened by almost 10 percent.

Cold Waves

When temperatures drop to very low levels within a day, it is called a cold wave. Such conditions can affect the daily routine of people. Cold waves normally occur every year in cold countries like the United States, Canada, and Russia. Now, with rising temperatures, the winter months are getting milder and cold waves have reduced. However, when they do occur, they are of an extreme nature and cause much death and damage.

Effects

During cold waves, people and animals die due to **hypothermia** and **frostbite**. Crop production suffers greatly. Water pipes freeze, causing serious damage to property. Reduction in **hydroelectricity** generation results in failure to meet the demand for electricity. Vehicles do not start in such extreme weather, thus affecting the transportation system. Fires become more dangerous as cold air contains more oxygen; once started, fires can become very intense.

Cold Hits United Kingdom and North America

Two examples of cold snaps: In mid-December 2009, a cold wave swept across the United Kingdom which led to a severe drop in temperatures during January 2010. The temperature slipped to –17.6 °C, making it the coldest January across the nation since 1987. In 2018, the United States and Canada suffered record-breaking cold, too. A "bomb cyclone" brought temperatures down to –90°F (–67°C) in New Hampshire. Boston got 15 feet (4.5 m) of snow.

Climate Facts

- During 1816, known as the "Year without a summer," global temperatures dropped to between 32-33°F (0.4-0.7 °C).

- During the 2018 cold snap, American weather was "upside down." One day, it was warmer in Alaska than it was in Florida.

Increasing Floods

G lobal warming has changed weather patterns and increased the risk of floods. The air becomes warm due to the increase in temperatures and holds more moisture. This can lead to floods during heavy rainfall. Changes in snowfall patterns and the melting of river ice have also increased the risk of floods.

Heavy Rainfall

A 1.44°F (0.8°C) increase in global temperatures causes the water vapor content in the air to increase by 3-4 percent. In the future, more and heavier rainfall is expected. Rivers would overflow, even destroying the barriers built to prevent flooding. Floods that have been occurring every twenty years in the Northeast and Midwestern United States are expected to occur every five years by the beginning of the next century.

Early Snowmelts

Another cause of frequent floods is the early melting of snow in the mountainous regions. For example, in the northwest region of the United States, snowmelt now occurs ten to twenty days earlier than it used to about fifty years ago. Many regions across the globe now experience rainfall instead of snow in winters. In the western United States, snowfall has decreased by about 10 percent since 1949. Melted snow, along with heavy rainfall, raises the water level of rivers, causing devastating floods.

Climate Facts

• In 2017, at least 41 million people were affected in floods in Bangladesh, India, and Nepal.

• Residents in Missouri, Nebraska, and Mississippi suffered through record flooding during the early spring of 2019.

2010 Pakistan Floods

n July 2010, Pakistan experienced the most disastrous rainfall in its history. Due to changing climate patterns, it started raining heavily in Sindh, Balochistan, and Khyber Pakhtunkhwa regions of Pakistan for a month. This caused **severe** floods, starting from the north and spreading all across the nation.

Causes

These destructive floods were caused due to global warming and the occurrence of **La Niña** (cooling of water) in the Pacific Ocean. Climate experts had already stated that climate change would cause abnormal and heavy rainfall in South Asia. The increase in the surface water temperature of the Bay of Bengal and the Mediterranean Sea caused the air to hold huge amounts of moisture. This caused heavy rainfall and made the Indus and Kabul Rivers overflow. In addition, the melted snow from the Karakoram Range added extra water to them.

Fatalities

One-fifth of the country's land area was flooded with water. **Innumerous** property was destroyed, including the famous Karakorum Highway that connected more than a half million people with the outside world. More than twenty million people were severely affected, and their properties destroyed. Around one thousand nine hundred people died and almost 8.5 million people lived in the open and in tents after the **calamity**.

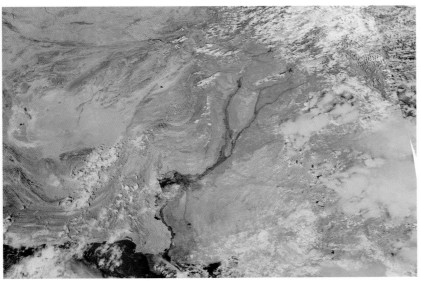

Climate Facts

• Pakistan was last hit by disastrous floods in 1929, but the damage caused was less as compared to the disaster caused by the 2010 floods.

• The 2010 monsoon in Pakistan recorded almost 86 percent more rainfall than usual.

Calamities in China

China has major industries that produce immense pollution and contribute to global warming. Due to the changing climate, extreme floods and droughts occurred in China in 2010 and 2011. The country suffered a major economic slowdown, huge numbers of deaths, and loss to infrastructure.

2010 Floods

These floods occurred in May and continued until September, affecting the twenty-eight provinces of the People's Republic of China (PRC), especially in the south. Floods and landslides killed about three thousand two hundred people. Around one thousand sixty people went missing in the disaster, more than two hundred thirty million were severely affected and their properties destroyed. The entire calamity caused a loss of around $52 billion.

2010–11 Drought

The most severe drought in the past 60 years began in September 2010, and affected eight provinces in the northern region, including those of Gansu, Hubei, Jiangsu, and Shaanxi. About 35 million people were severely affected and by June 2011, about 4.2 million faced a shortage of drinking water. The country suffered a loss of $2.3 billion due to the calamity.

Billion-Dollar Disasters

The impact of climate change continues to be felt in China. In 2018, the country suffered seven weather disasters that each did more than $1 billion in damage. Typhoon Mangkhut was one of the worst, creating more than $6 billion of damage to mainland China and Hong Kong, as well as adversely affecting the Philippines. Summer flooding in central China killed 89 people and destroyed more than $5 billion worth of property.

Climate Facts

- In the 2010 China floods, about 37,500 sq. mi. (97,000 sq km) of harvest were flooded.

- Around 35 percent of China's total wheat produce was destroyed in the 2010–11 drought. As a result, global wheat prices shot up in early 2011.

Hurricanes

Hurricanes are very strong tropical storms that form above the eastern Pacific and Atlantic oceans. Strong winds with a speed higher than 75 mph (120 kph) blow during a hurricane, and there is an excessive amount of rainfall that leads to heavy floods.

Hurricane Katrina, 2005

In August 2005, the United States encountered its worst hurricane. It caused damages worth $125 billion to the country. Around one thousand eight hundred thirty people died. The areas severely affected by the hurricane included Alabama, south Florida, Louisiana, Mississippi, a major part of eastern North America, and the Bahamas.

New York Times: After Katrina

Effects Due to Changing Climate

Hurricanes get their energy from warm oceans. Due to global warming, the ocean temperatures have risen by 1.44°F (0.8°C) since 1970. Some recent studies have noted that since the 1970s, hurricanes have become extremely powerful and their duration has also increased by almost 50 percent.

Future

On the one hand, the wind speed of Atlantic **cyclones** is expected to increase by 3–11 percent by the end of the twenty-first century. As a result, the number of the strongest hurricanes would double. Heavy rainfall would also increase by about 22 percent within 62 miles (100 km) of the hurricane. On the other hand, the number of tropical hurricanes would decline by 23 percent in the western Pacific region.

Climate Facts

- Hurricanes are popularly known as cyclones in the Southern Hemisphere and typhoons in the Western Pacific.

- Led by Hurricane Florence, which hit Florida, the 2018 North American hurricane season was one of the worst on record.

Thunderstorms

Natural events such as thunderstorms occur when there is warm air near the ground and cold air much above the surface. Winds rise from below with great strength, causing storms. Water vapor also rises due to evaporation, forming clouds. This causes heavy rainfall and lightning. Approximately one thousand eight hundred thunderstorms occur daily worldwide, but global warming is severely increasing their frequency and intensity.

Effects of Global Warming

Scientists have observed that with rising global temperatures, there would be an increase in the humid air that causes the formation of thunderstorms. Although the powerful winds that add to the storms would decrease, the humid air would offset the decrease in winds, leading to more severe thunderstorms. Extreme thunderstorms would increase during the seasonal period, causing more destruction than ever.

2010 Western Australian Storms

In March 2010, a severe thunderstorm struck Western Australia. It was accompanied by baseball-sized **hail**, heavy rainfall, and strong winds that caused massive damage to cars and property. It was the most damaging thunderstorm in Western Australia's history, causing destruction worth almost $1.08 billion. Lightning caused power failure in about 157,500 houses.

Climate Facts

- A thunderstorm is severe when the hail is 1.9 cm in diameter and the winds reach a speed of 58 mph.

- In the Midwestern and Southern states of the United States, almost one hundred thousand thunderstorms occur every year.

Droughts

A drought is a period when the weather becomes extremely dry and there is a severe shortage of water. Droughts occur in many parts of the world every year. However, due to extreme weather conditions, they are becoming more severe in areas that already face them. Droughts now occur even in those regions that never faced them earlier.

Classification

- When the **precipitation** in a certain area is less than normal, it is called a meteorological drought.
- When there is a deficiency in surface and underground water, it is called a hydrological drought.
- When there is a decrease in soil moisture and the soil is unable to sustain a crop, it is called an agricultural drought.
- When the shortage of water starts affecting people and causing deaths, it is called a socioeconomic drought.

Drought Patterns

According to the Intergovernmental Panel on Climate Change (IPCC), scientists have stated that climate change is, to some extent, responsible for changing the drought patterns worldwide. However, they have refused to identify any single pattern. There are parts of Europe and Africa that are becoming drier. On the other hand, in North America, droughts have become less frequent and less severe.

Future

According to some recent studies, if the Earth continues to heat up, droughts are likely to intensify in the Mediterranean, Central America, Mexico, northeast Brazil, and southern Africa. Drier regions may experience longer periods of drought. This will have a major impact on agriculture and wildlife.

Climate Facts

- Long periods of drought in the Horn of Africa have led to a severe food crisis affecting ten million people.

- The United States suffers an annual loss of about $7–8 billion due to droughts.

Extreme Droughts

Soaring temperatures around the globe are causing extreme droughts in various locations at a given time. Some of the worst droughts have occurred in the last few years, causing more deaths than ever before. Drought-prone countries, such as those in Africa, are facing some of the most severe droughts due to global warming.

2010 Amazon Rainforests

In 2010, the southwestern Amazon basin, two regions in northern Bolivia, and the Brazilian state of Mato Grosso, were hit by one of the worst droughts in a hundred years. About 57 percent of the Amazon area had less rainfall. Normally, the Amazon forests absorb about 1.5 gigatons of carbon dioxide (CO_2) annually, but due to the large-scale death of trees, about eight gigatons of CO_2 stored underground was released. This further contributed to global warming.

2010 Sahel

Africa's Sahel region was hit by severe drought in June–August 2010. Temperatures in the Chad region rose to 117°F (47.6°C) and reached as high as 121°F (49.6°C) in Sudan. The region's crop production failed, bringing about one of the worst **famines** in its history, and leading 17.5 million people to starvation. The 2012 Sahel drought furthered this food crisis, leaving 18.7 million people at risk of starvation.

Droughts Continued in 2018

Several areas of the world experienced extreme drought through 2018 and into 2019. Farmers in Argentina lost nearly $4 billion as a nearly two-year-long drought continued. Drought conditions in the southwest United States and California were finally eased by rain and snow in late 2018, but many communities continued to have reserves far below normal. In Australia, cows and sheep were dying by the thousands as drought and heat plagued most of the center of the country.

Climate Facts

- In the 2010 drought, the water levels of the Amazon River were the lowest since 1963.

- The Australian drought was called in 2018 by some farmers "the worst in all of our recorded memories."

Severe Wildfires

Forests are very **susceptible** to fires during the summer months. Once a wildfire starts, it becomes uncontrollable, causing large-scale destruction and pollution. Since the 1980s, spring seasons are getting warmer and the summers are getting longer. Such changes in climate are making wildfires more intense.

Drier Conditions

Rising temperatures are increasing the drier conditions in dry regions; this, in turn, increases the chances of fire occurrences. By mid-century, an increase of between 4 and 8°F (2.2 and 4.4°C) in summer temperatures in western North America is expected. This would increase the evaporation rate and decrease precipitation by almost 16 percent.

More Beetles

Global warming is increasing the number of insects and beetles, which survive longer in warmer conditions. They infest the forests even in the winter season, and increase the number of dead trees that act as fuel for wildfires, as they rapidly catch and spread fire.

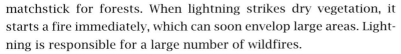

Lightning

Global warming has increased the number and severity of thunderstorms. Lightning during a thunderstorm acts as a burning matchstick for forests. When lightning strikes dry vegetation, it starts a fire immediately, which can soon envelop large areas. Lightning is responsible for a large number of wildfires.

Climate Facts

- In August 2012, a raging fire on the forested Greek island of Chios burned tens of thousands of acres of forest.

- About $1 billion is spent annually for firefighting purposes in the United States.

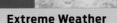

Wildfires Around the World

orest fires occur around the world, destroying the habitats of numerous wild animals and causing vast air pollution. Rising temperatures are increasing the incidences and intensity of wildfires everywhere. They are severely affecting people's health and causing huge economic losses.

2010 Russia

In 2010, as the temperature in Russia rose up to 98°F (37°C), it caused about 1,200 wildfires. The smoke from the fires caused smog all around, forcing Russian President Dmitry Medvedev to declare an **emergency** in Mordovia, Moscow, Ryazan, Vladimir, and Voronezh. Around 310,000 acres (125,500 hectares) of land were burned in the wildfires and 34 people were killed. About 86,000 people were forced to leave their homes for safety reasons.

2010 Bolivia Forest Fires

Starting in August 2010, more than twenty-five thousand wildfires occurred in Bolivia, burning about 3.7 million acres (1.5 million hectares). The fire was started by farmers to expand their agricultural land. Due to extremely hot conditions, the fire spread across the country, forcing the government to declare an emergency.

2009 Australian Bushfires

From February 7 to March 14, 2009, around 400 wild bushfires occurred in Victoria, Australia. It happened because the temperature rose up to 115.5°F (46.4°C). More than 170 people were killed in the disaster and about 415 were severely injured. A total area of 1,718 square miles (4,451 sq. km) was burned and the damage caused was approximately worth $1 billion.

Australian bush fire aftermath

Climate Facts

- The Russian wildfires caused damage of about $15 billion.

- In 1983, 76 people died in the wildfire of Victoria and South Australia. They are also called the "Ash Wednesday" fires.

Extreme Allergies

Global warming is affecting humans in many ways. Common allergies among people are increasing because of rising temperatures. Changing climate is affecting the pollen season and the growth of other **allergens** around the world.

Ragweed Pollen

Warmer climate makes ragweed plants grow faster and for longer periods. They are the main source of pollens that cause fall **hay fever**. These plants tend to have more allergenic content when the atmosphere has higher CO_2 levels. Now they produce almost double the number of pollens in autumn than they did about 100 years ago. This has greatly increased the number of allergies among people.

Tree Pollen

During spring, people suffer from allergies caused by tree **pollens**. Rising temperatures help the growth of allergenic trees, such as hickories and oaks. Since the spring season has started arriving almost two weeks earlier than it did about twenty years ago, **pollination** in trees begins earlier, resulting in an increase in allergies.

Asthma on the Rise

Asthma is a disease of the respiratory system, in which the airways swell making it difficult to breathe. Higher temperatures and excess of CO_2 in the atmosphere are making the allergy seasons worse by helping plants to produce more pollen and increasing the growth of fungi. Rising temperatures also lead to an increase in the ground-level ozone (smog) production, posing a serious threat to asthmatics.

 Climate Facts

- According to studies, the total seasonal pollen for many plants, such as ragweed, is increasing due to warming.

- Increased CO_2 levels in the air help the growth of poison ivy, affecting about three million five hundred thousand people every year in the United States.

Landslides, Mudslides, & Avalanches

With each passing year, rising temperatures are increasing rain in some areas to an extreme level, in turn bringing about floods. This has greatly increased the number of landslides, mudslides, and avalanches, causing more deaths than any other disaster.

Landslide

A landslide is the flow of rocks, land, and debris from the slope of a mountain, mostly set off by **prolonged** rainfall or excessive rainfall over a short period of time. Every year almost one thousand people die in landslides. From 2007 to 2010, almost 12,000 deaths were caused due to landslides in about seventy countries. Data from 2017 shows the problem continues, as more than 4,000 people were killed that year. A landslide in Sierra Leone was responsible for more than 1,100 of those deaths.

Mudslide

A mudslide is the flow of a huge mass of loose mud from a hill, containing 30 percent of water, at a speed of 50 mph (80 kph). It is mostly set off by sudden heavy rainfall or excessive snowmelt. In December 1999, heavy rains caused a mudslide in Venezuela, affecting an area up to 37 miles (60 km) and killing about 30,000 people. About 85,000 people were evacuated and the event caused $3.5 billion of damage. In 2018, 23 people died near Santa Barbara, California, when massive mudslides roared down hills scarred by recent wildfires.

Avalanche

Huge amounts of snow, rocks, and ice run down the hill at a great speed in an avalanche. This occurs when there is external pressure on the standing snow by way of excessive rain or snowfall, or when there is a rapid increase in temperature, which makes it weak and sets off an avalanche. The largest avalanche occurred in 1962 on the Huascaran Mountain in Peru, spreading up to nine miles and killing more than 6,000 people.

Climate Facts

- In the last century, out of 500 landslides, 220 occurred in Asia alone.

- In 2002, an avalanche of twenty million tons occurred from Mount Kazbek in Caucasus, killing more than 145 people.

Winter Weather

Global warming is affecting the summer as well as the winter climate in a great way. While summer months are becoming severe, winter months are becoming milder and shorter with each passing year. The weather conditions in winters are no longer as predictable as they were about twenty years ago.

Unpredictable Winters

Winter months are shrinking as the spring season begins about fifteen days early everywhere. In some areas, winters are getting milder. However, scientists studying climate change have predicted extreme winters in Britain and the rest of Northern Europe due to the melting of the Arctic Sea ice. Heavy snowfall and snowstorms are also becoming common in some parts of the world during the winter months.

Effect on Ecosystem

The number of diseases and pests are increasing due to shorter and milder winters. The tremendous increase of pine bark beetles in the mountains of the western United States is one example. The ticks that carry **Lyme disease** and survive only in warm weather are also increasing. Plant production like that of cherries and walnuts suffers because they require cold conditions for proper growth.

Effect on Economy

Winter **recreational** activities that are a major source of revenue for many countries are affected due to global warming. The $66 billion ski industry in the United States has started facing losses due to shorter winters, more rains, and less snowfall. Ice fishing in the Midwest is also decreasing as rivers freeze later and the ice is dangerously thin.

Climate Facts

• Since 1949, snowfall has decreased by about 9 percent in the Western United States and by 22 percent in the Northeast United States.

• In early 2019, media reports called the massive snowfall across Europe the worst snow disaster on the continent in more than 30 years.

Glacial Earthquakes

Increasing temperature is causing the rapid movement of glaciers, which results in glacial earthquakes. Their magnitude is as high as 5.1 on the moment magnitude scale. They mainly occur in the regions of Alaska, Antarctica, and Greenland.

How Do They Occur?

Glaciers are huge chunks of ice that move slowly into the sea. However, due to global warming they are moving rapidly. Once the melted water reaches the base, it makes the glaciers slip quickly. The weight of these glaciers puts pressure on the crust of the earth and as they slip away, the pressure is released in the form of earthquakes. The **tremors** of these quakes are felt in regions up to 4,125 miles (6,440 km) away.

Effect of Global Warming

Scientists have noted that the number of glacial earthquakes has increased because of the rapid movement of Greenland's huge ice blocks. They mainly occur in the summer months when ice melts quickly due to global warming. Scientists found that the quakes' frequency was increasing through 2013. As many as half the total number of earthquakes happened in the final two years of the study.

St. Elias Earthquake

According to scientists, the 1979 St. Elias earthquake in southern Alaska occurred due to the quick melting of glaciers in the area. The quake had a magnitude of 7.2 on the moment magnitude scale.

National Geographic: Earthquakes

Climate Facts

- In northwestern Greenland, only one earthquake had occurred from 1993 to 1999; but from 2000 to 2005, more than 24 quakes were recorded.

- A part of the Whillans Ice Stream in Antarctica moves by 2.2 feet (0.67 m) in almost 25 minutes, twice a day, into the Ross Sea Ice Shelf.

A Disastrous 2018

The year 2018 was remarkable for the high number of extreme weather events. It was among the hottest years every recorded, but it was also a time of many specific weather disasters. These disasters killed many people, and affected millions more. Are they a sign of things to come?

More Heat Records

Japan suffered through record-breaking heat that hospitalized more than 22,000 people. In Algeria, a new continental record for Africa was set when the thermometer reached 124°F (51.1°C). NOAA reported that the average summer temperature for the United States was the highest since records began in 1895. Every one of the 50 states had higher-than-average minimum summer readings.

Deadly Wildfires

California has often suffered wildfires. In 2018, however, it had its worst yet. The Camp Fire killed 85 people and destroyed more than 15,000 structures. Damage estimates were a shocking $16.5 billion. The town of Paradise in northern California was almost completely destroyed by a fast-moving blaze. Another effect of the fires was an increase in debris flow and mudslides after heavy rains. The fires burned off plants that held soil. When rains poured, the soil was washed off. In one instance near Santa Barbara, 22 people were killed in minutes by a sudden debris flow.

Carbon Dioxide Record

Even as the Paris Agreement steered nations toward reducing emissions, scientists reported that carbon dioxide poured into the atmosphere at a record level in 2018. The rate of increase from 2017 was 2.6 percent; the rate had gone up in 2017 as well.

Climate Facts

• In 2018, Hurricane Michael smashed into Florida with record-setting winds.

• Along with heat, Japan had flooding in 2018 that led to 5 million people evacuating.

Environmental Refugees

Refugees are people who are forced to change their homelands because of political, religious, and other reasons. Environmental refugees are those who leave their homes because of natural or man-made disasters like earthquakes, hurricanes, deforestation, and **desertification**. Since the frequency of natural disasters is increasing every year, the number of global environmental refugees is also increasing.

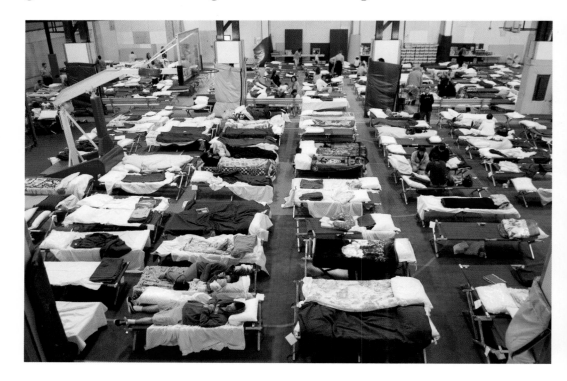

Three Types

There are three types of environmental refugees:

- Those who leave their homes for a short period due to a **disruption** in their residing location.
- Those who leave their homes due to poor conditions in their residing locations. Coastal degradation, deforestation, and other causes may lead to such movement.
- Those who wish to resettle to avoid problems and changes in their habitat.

Environmental Refugees Worldwide

According to the UN Refugee Agency in 2016, there has been an annual increase in 21.5 million environmental refugees per year. Their total number is expected to reach 200 million by 2050. About two million refugees were living in Mexico, escaping environmental degradation; almost 15 million refugees were taking refuge in sub-Saharan Africa while fleeing droughts, and the remaining refugees were living in Central America, China, and the Indian subcontinent.

Climate Facts

- Lester Brown, a US environmental analyst, coined the term "environmental refugee" in 1976.

- Environmental refugees do not get any legal aid. However, they are given access to food, shelter, monetary grants, clinics, and schools.

1. Where was a deadly heat wave in 2003?

2. Name one specific cause of the increase in severity of floods.

3. What hurricane struck the southern United States in 2005?

4. What is a drought?

5. What type of insect is increasing in number rapidly in forests due to wildfires?

6. What disease is on the rise due to increased pollen in the air?

7. What is a glacier?

8. What does the text describe as the site of terrible wildfires in 2018?

1. Keep a weather log of your area for a month. Note temperature, precipitation, and other weather events. Research your area and compare your results to a similar list from past years. Do you see any changes?

2. Pick one of the weather disasters mentioned in the text and do further research. What were the main causes of the event? How did it affect people? What changes were made to help reduce the impact of future, similar events?

3. Many communities encourage people to prepare for emergencies. Ask your local authorities or do research online and help your family build an emergency kit. What materials should you have in it? How can it be stored? What basic needs must be met?

Books

Hirsch, Rebecca. *Climate Migrants: On the Move in a Warming World.* Mankato, MN: Twenty-First Century Books, 2016.

Lusted, Marcia Amidon. *Extreme Weather Events (Global Viewpoints).* Farmington Hills, MI: Greenhaven Press, 2017.

Kostigen, Thomas M. *Extreme Weather: Surviving Tornadoes, Sandstorms, Hailstorms, Blizzards, Hurricanes, and More!* Washington, D.C.: National Geographic Childrens, 2014.

On the Internet

World Resource Institute/Extreme Weather
www.wri.org/blog/2018/12/2018-year-climate-extremes

Union of Concerned Scientists
www.ucsusa.org/global-warming/science-and-impacts/impacts/extreme-weather-climate-change.html

Scientific American
www.scientificamerican.com/article/climate-change-and-extreme-weather/

bioaccumulation the process of the buildup of toxic chemical substances in the body

biodiversity the diversity of plant and animal life in a habitat (or in the world as a whole)

ecosystem refers to a community of organisms, their interaction with each other, and their physical environment

famine a severe shortage of food (as through crop failure), resulting in hunger, starvation, and death

hydrophobic tending to repel, and not absorb water or become wet by water

irrigation the method of providing water to agricultural fields

La Niña periodic, significant cooling of the surface waters of the equatorial Pacific Ocean, which causes abnormal weather patterns

migration the movement of persons or animals from one country or locality to another

pollutants the foreign materials which are harmful to the environment

precipitation the falling to earth of any form of water (rain, snow, hail, sleet, or mist)

stressors processes or events that cause stress

susceptible yielding readily to or capable of

symbiotic the interaction between organisms (especially of different species) that live together and happen to benefit from each other

vulnerable someone or something that can be easily harmed or attacked

INDEX

Photo Credits

Photographs sourced by Macaw Media, except for: Dreamstime.com: Woyzzeck 23T; ChelseaSuzanne 31T; Elziveta Galitskaya 32; Bennymarty 39T; Shutterstock: Mihai Bogdan-Lazar 40; Felix Lipov 41T; Abramov Michael 41B.